T0038753

S
K
E
L
E
T
O
N
S

ALSO BY DEBORAH LANDAU

Soft Targets

The Uses of the Body

The Last Usable Hour

Orchidelirium

DEBORAH LANDAU

SKELETONS

COPPER CANYON PRESS
PORT TOWNSEND, WASHINGTON

Copyright 2023 by Deborah Landau
All rights reserved
Printed in the United States of America

Cover artwork by Anita Huffington, *Moonrise*, 2003. Alabaster, 15 × 7¼ × 7½ inches.
Credit © 2022 Anita Huffington. Courtesy of ACA Galleries, NY.
www.anitahuffington.com

Copper Canyon Press is in residence at Fort Worden State Park in Port Townsend,
Washington, under the auspices of Centrum. Centrum is a gathering place for artists
and creative thinkers from around the world, students of all ages and backgrounds, and
audiences seeking extraordinary cultural enrichment.

LIBRARY OF CONGRESS CATALOGING-IN-PUBLICATION DATA
Names: Landau, Deborah, Ph.D., author.
Title: Skeletons / Deborah Landau.
Description: Port Townsend, Washington : Copper Canyon Press, ⌊2023⌋ |
    Summary: "A collection of poems by Deborah Landau"—Provided by
    publisher.
Identifiers: LCCN 2022046010 (print) | LCCN 2022046011 (ebook) |
    ISBN 9781556596650 (paperback) | ISBN 9781619322677 (epub)
Subjects: LCGFT: Poetry.
Classification: LCC PS3612.A54755 S54 2023 (print) |
    LCC PS3612.A54755 (ebook) | DDC 811/.6—dc23/eng/20220928
LC record available at https://lccn.loc.gov/2022046010
LC ebook record available at https://lccn.loc.gov/2022046011

98765432 FIRST PRINTING

COPPER CANYON PRESS
Post Office Box 271
Port Townsend, Washington 98368

www.coppercanyonpress.org

ACKNOWLEDGMENTS

Thank you to the editors of the following publications, in which versions of poems from this collection originally appeared:

The Nation: Skeletons ("Skeleton, some wonder," "Sorry not sorry, said death," and "Sunday sloth is its own milk and honey")

The New Yorker: Ecstasies ("Catch me alive? I am today—"), Flesh ("The long and short of it"), Skeletons ("So whatever's the opposite of a Buddhist," "Summer dark found us," and "Sundays I spend feeling sorry for myself")

The New York Review of Books: Skeleton ("Streaming Netflix")

Plume: Skeleton ("Shabbier I am still")

Poetry: Flesh ("Every bliss is built this way" and "To be kissed?"), Skeletons ("Superluminal travel isn't possible," "Soporifics fail tonight," and "Should we get a dog?")

The Yale Review: Skeletons ("Spooky, everyone under their face," "Strutting avec Cyndi Lauper," and "Sugar withdrawal symptoms")

The Best American Poetry 2022: Skeletons ("So whatever's the opposite of a Buddhist" and "Sundays I spend feeling sorry for myself")

My gratitude to the dear friends who read this book as I wrote it. Warmest thanks, as always, to my stellar editor, Michael Wiegers, and to everyone at Copper Canyon Press.

for Mark

CONTENTS

SKELETONS

3   So whatever's the opposite of a Buddhist

4   Sundays I spend feeling sorry for myself

5   Superluminal travel isn't possible

6   Serenity, that's a vicious circular one.

FLESH

9   It must give pleasure

SKELETONS

11   Sugar withdrawal symptoms

12   Strutting avec Cyndi Lauper

13   Sunday sloth is its own milk and honey

14   Shaken I download "Aura"

FLESH

17   To be kissed?

SKELETONS

19   Sex came from nowhere

20   Soon we were enthralled

21   Sorry not sorry, said death.

22   Surprises weren't really our thing

FLESH

25   To be afraid of every edge

SKELETONS

27 Streaming Netflix

28 Soporifics fail tonight

29 S'mores aren't vegetarian

30 Studmuffin stuntman

FLESH

33 Every bliss is built this way

SKELETONS

35 Sucker punched this morning

36 Should we get a dog?

37 Silence isn't viable tonight

38 Stolen year but we're still here.

FLESH

41 Kissing his cheek.

SKELETONS

43 She tended to ruminate

44 Spooky, everyone under their face

45 Scrooge-morning after Halloween

46 Stumbled into a new context today

FLESH

49 I thought a lot about your body

SKELETONS

51 Savasana pose we kept practicing

52 Sorry to text so late

53 Shabbier I am still

54 So after a year undercover

FLESH

57 The long and short of it

SKELETONS

59 Summer dark found us

60 Sexing sunburned

61 Slot-machine cherries

62 Skeleton, some wonder

FLESH

65 You in your ecstasy of coffee

66 I wanted to write the thing itself—

67 It wouldn't be so bad

ECSTASIES

69 In the xyzs of nights and days

70 Like most people

71 Are we done with life?

72 Even coffins oblige

73 Catch me alive? I am today—

74 ABOUT THE AUTHOR

S
K
E
L
E
T
O
N
S

SKELETON

So whatever's the opposite of a Buddhist that's what I am.

Kindhearted, yes, but knee-deep in existential gloom,

except when the fog smokes the bridges like this—

like, instead of being afraid, we might juice ourselves up,

eh, like, might get kissed again? Dwelling in bones I go straight

through life, a sublime abundance—cherries, dog's breath, the sun, then

(ouch) & all of us snuffed out. Dear one, what is waiting for us tonight,

nostalgia? the homes of childhood? oblivion? How we hate to go—

SKELETON

Sundays I spend feeling sorry for myself I've got a
knack for it I'm morbid, make the worst of any season
exclamation point   yet levity's a liquor of sorts,
lowers us through life toward the terminus soon
extinguished   darling, the comfort is slight,
tucked in bed we search each other for some alternative—
oh let's marvel at the world, the stroke and colors of it
now, while breathing.

SKELETON

Superluminal travel isn't possible for humans, you said. It seemed

karmic. We were running toward abundance as if our livesdependedonit,

egads, but never fast enough.   To fermata the present

lacuna was another way.   An opposite approach—

embrace this day.   *You are transitory,*

the world laughed.   Oh yeah, we laughed back. So what?

Ovulating, while it lasted, was a blast, mainlining that Eros—

nectar, nabbed.   (As if!)   Any way outta this bag of bones?

SKELETON

Serenity, that's a vicious circular one. I've tried loving

kindness, chocolate, running at night, vitality,

energy drinks, slacking on a terrace in Paris, deep breath,

lilacs, trying to chill out, what a joke. It don't last long.

Everything dulls to a fugue state, its singular pulsing

tremor, its lack of friction. Yet persists such capacity to feel alive,

oceanic in my longing for rain, for the end of me, fluidity, freedom—

numinous the world glowing on without us its golden hours and shady graves.

FLESH

It must give pleasure but rarely it rarely does.

But pleasure is so useful when it comes.

Pleasure says this is your sort of place, your year, you live here.

Pleasure's the perfect swerve. It wins you back.

Pain won't take you nowhere.

Chocolate on the tongue. Vodka. Velvet. Voilà.

A zipper slinking in its silver, its long slide down.

SKELETON

Sugar withdrawal symptoms turn out to be what, exactly—

keto flu, depression, killer headaches & cravings   (cravings) (cravings)

endorphins how I long for you—   longing, that's a sugar &

love is,   morning sun too, especially through open windows &

earth is a sugar while it still greens around us. What else sweetens? Not

the internet, not tweets, except Alex's (poems in tweets' clothing), definitely not

one (a tweet) from the president   yet iced with the season's first

narcissus blooms this day, & somehow it's still a thrill to wake, warmbodied alive

SKELETON

Strutting avec Cyndi Lauper, a flourish.   Stunt-

kissing Kevin S. behind school on roller skates   getting all

electric in biology class, at Dairy Queen, babysitting, Eric M.

lying on top of me under layers of Michigan winter   we were

excessive.   Those scenarios could get orthodontically complex.

Trepidatious afterglow we'd saunter back to school. Who needed

oratory? We were mad for the body in its meant-for-pleasure finery, lips a-cherry,

nails glossed wine, libido an overdrive meant to keep us here a long time.

SKELETON

Sunday sloth is its own milk and honey, honey, am I right?

Kudos to you for rationalizing your lazy ass again as in,

er, "not writing is also writing." Pussycat, I have bad news.

Lethargy is for losers. *Be kind to yourself,* the shrink said. I felt shrunk.

Enervating this dopamine addiction and tendency to

toggle between gloomy and elate. Yeah, one minute she's

ogling men on the metro like some grody monsieur, the next wanting to die.

Natch, dear, you're here! Don't ruin everything, for god's sake.

SKELETON

Shaken I download "Aura" and "Calm" to quell my

kvetch—what if? what if?—after midnight it verges

extreme. *In this moment you are safe* says app lady, handoverheart.

Let's say that's true, hm.　　　　Does mantra work as

explodes the tunnel and the train fills with fire?

Top-heavy ruminations send me spiraling again

oy vey decimating yet another night. Can't sleep.

Now for some music, try some dancing? Nah. Still blue.

FLESH

To be kissed? Waiter!
I like watching you
sliding into the banquette
with a red wine
a warm glass
still animate
only flesh is elevating it clasps
a prick can be key
how it brings along
exquisite its red life animal press
dark between bones
like the body's answer
to the doozy of us
hurled forward
still talking all spent
& always dizzying near
with sour breath
time's metric shhhh

SKELETON

Sex came from nowhere an illogic

kind of fracture   a heat in the element

edging fires stirred until they

lit the towns to one another   carrying us

ever forward in flesh   together & through

this fever leads   an audience of dog gathers

oohlala   ah stop (silly isn't hot)   well,

namaste! It was on a lark it was for the moment we tried each thing.

SKELETON

Soon we were enthralled, engaged, en route to

Kleinfeld's, it was hard to find a dress, submit,

embrace the schlock. A bride was always already empty, a circumstance.

Lace made me itch. A fabric trap. The 10,000 buttons. The kitsch.

Everything trending toward what, exactly?

Teetering along together we felt rather, reeling toward the altar eyes

open, eyes shut. Never better, we said, as the guests arrived. We went full-on

nuptial. He and She. The moon filled up, took its last drink of the sea.

SKELETON

Sorry not sorry, said death. He wasn't fucking around, incessant

klepto. Meanwhile, the internets wouldn't shut up about perfection,

elegance, the feminine ideal, that old regime. It was hard not to puff up while

lactating. It took heft to host the parasite. Pregnancy brought a swampy

edema. Bye-bye, ankles. Nice knowing you, feet. Intermittent fasting?

Time to give it a rest.   We shrink eventual to the ultimate bone,

obits keening, farewell, flesh! So wax zaftig, carb while you can, willy-

nilly you'll get there, we'll get there together, we're already on our way.

SKELETON

Surprises weren't really our thing, the brightness,

keeping it to ourselves for a while felt right.

Elation or shock? A bit of both, two parents on a plank

leaving nature to its ripening. We liked birth, it kept the death away—

each time one kid grew we'd hatch another

talisman to fasten down the day.

Oblivious, true, our delirium made you.

(Never thought we'd lapse like this, but phew.)

FLESH

To be afraid of every edge, the falling off of it.
Walking at night. Walking under the scaffolding,
passing the spot where the kid lost his phone at gunpoint,
where my daughter while walking to school past the trash
and daffodils was actually in the moment truly happy.
How mildly the days go by and again
the small cove, after the workday, of going home.
This day. The next. The great lengths we went to save
the wild turkeys last summer, how the traffic stopped for them
while the factory farms fed each and every chick
chick chick chick chick into the chipper.

SKELETON

Streaming Netflix is the opposite of action, a nap
kept low-burning on the margins as if not
existing I don't exist   slipped from the yoke of life simple
lazy the hours pass until the active life, its people and tethers
ether-wisp into a faint of memory, a trace. The small art and craft of
talk, how did we manage it? Some things stayed the same, like
our nostalgia, like insomnia. Faraway places became more like this place.
Nights were felt as a stream of departures in the hive.

SKELETON

Soporifics fail tonight   nerves scuttling in the
kitchen   god-knows-what skulking round in its nasty restless
exoskeleton. It seems we're creeping into the midnight of our fleeting
lives. Avarice, nasty, snark all trending . . . nothing so fuzzy or
elemental as love.   Is this the new new age? *Do not
touch* said the calendar on every single page.
On with it, life said.   One day we'll all just zoom away.
(Now I've put too fine a point on it.)

SKELETON

S'mores aren't vegetarian but let's leave that out of it,

kibosh, shush up 'bout the gelatin factories, lighten up now,

extra marshmallows please. We attempted festive, desperate

limbo year, camped on the roof lit illegal in the firepit flare.

Errant nights as in anything-can-happen, caged days

traipsing round the living room streaming a cringey dance class

oblivious to the rearview photobomb, the dogs joining in, our

nonstop stopped. *It's the end of New York,* Z said.

SKELETON

Studmuffin stuntman spicing up my winter quarantine

keep out of my dreams please with your

ersatz bedside manner inciting my time-wasting

libidinous should-we-get-to-know-each-other in some deep

ecstatic way?   um, don't confuse dreamy apparition with

true tonic   wilding into ruminative loop-the-loops—

ok, let's bring it down a notch   say yes to hot earthling

nirvana—the incarnate husband, mortalflesh here&now

FLESH

Every bliss is built this way, a hollow thing,

with many entrances, with blood pumping

a live tongue and limber torso, a fine sweat rising in.

We dirty ourselves up. We leave our print.

The night sky 'tis a lozenge that cuts through the larded mind.

How I am inside I can scarce encompass it.

Eros sleeps with the windows open to uncoffin the room,

the wind blowing across the bed, trees scarecrowing the sky.

Congratulations. You scored a heat.

It's safe to say we lived for this back then.

In Berkeley, Ann Arbor, Gowanus—

Eros travels everywhere in its morphine case.

And again our clothes are on the floor.

Did you come? I am hiding behind this language.

What if I just went and said it

direct face-to-face unblushing.

SKELETON

Sucker punched this morning by someone's nostalgic yacht-rock playlist

kvelling a bit (memories!)   trying to generate a little life fizz

energy-burst. Clickbait lipstick? Rush into the city like the city still exists?

Lately days dull into a corner where we sit with our coffee

endless gibbous squinting at screens without ever

touching the sweatered shoulder of a friend or looking into her irl eyes—

ouch this isolation it burns yet I still love virtual you

nether-headed as we all are anyway   aren't we?

SKELETON

Should we get a dog? We talked about it for blocks.

Klutzes, what wouldwedo with a puppy? You with your

edibles and me kinda losing my mind.

Look at us here, stranded.   Long weekend? The longest.

Evidently we've been cultivating a deliberate recklessness,

trapped in this getaway for what seems like

oblivion.   Are you for real? It's a marvelous toxin, shut in

narcotic in these parentheses, nodding off together one breath at a time.

SKELETON

Silence isn't viable tonight   our foul country's widening

kiss   all our lips

ensconced now   and we are effing

livid   what life was   remember?

ecocide   we're on the brink of it still sleeping

tell me   no good   foul-mouthed

oaf of clumsiness   oh she is in a mood   no

nuance to this I realize, apologies

SKELETON

Stolen year but we're still here. Meditation fails,

kabbalah perplexes, a gloom fouls the stacked weeks—

emojis can't put a dent in it.   Astral mysteries script our

lives, or so they say.   I must have forgotten to post an update.

Ennui sets in and in and in.

Thaws a little then freezes.   Rinse, repeat.

Obvs I've bungled things again. About last

night? We might have gotten a bit too tipsy, it's true.

FLESH

Kissing his cheek. Swallowing water. An orgasm.

Blooms on the nightstand. Too many peaches to eat.

A bit of that drench. A residue.

Can't reenact though we try and try.

Ecstasy belongs to the past, when twenty,

when back then, when all-out and youth burn.

A lyrical time. I revisit it in dreams

as one who's abdicated.

As the purest once-lapsed nun.

SKELETON

She tended to ruminate, spawning sad

kinda plaintive poems   as if the poem wanted a friend to

eat dinner with, as if the poem were afraid of being alone all its

life.   DL, what's wrong with you, stuck in the dense

echo chamber of your head allthetime. *You seem like a lively person,*

T said, *though your poems are so bleak.*

Oof that's like when a man calls out *smile*

now sunshine as you walk down the street.

SKELETON

Spooky, everyone under their face seems to be

kaput   know what I mean?

Excessive sprawl of generations emptying onward

labile, fleeting   then that's it forever, bang.

Eager to stay, I take the kale and kombucha

toting a calamitous hairdo and wrecked face as

onward we sublimate (bones, bones, bones)

never again veiled in skin.

SKELETON

Scrooge-morning after Halloween trick-or-treating canceled

kids fretting but making the best of it & on to November's

election what a week this is   what a landlocked year

lauding the mess of life back before times

elusive now   dinners, movies, canoodling & such.

(Tsk miss tachycardia, you've too much time to think.

Oxygenate, they say calm waters run underneath—

now exhale, that's it, dip your ladle in & drink.)

SKELETON

Stumbled   into a new context today   feeling

kinesthetic dopamine abundance as though (is this joy?)

eviscerating the void   a fresh sugar grounding

lushest life, the true mouth in sweetest opposition to the endless

endlessness into which (we disappear)   begs the tongue to differ, says

this is raspberry, this cocoa, this the tender flesh

of peach, says a body I am and right now it's fine with me, it's copacetic.

Nothing we'll be nothing, *nothing* forever?

FLESH

I thought a lot about your body, my body,
what it is to lie in bed together and sleep.
To the shores of silent-dark and back
we went each night, like that wasn't a mystery.
Our physicality grew more hulking.
More and more I had to squint at the mirror
to recognize my face, that cracked window.

SKELETON

Savasana pose we kept practicing in vain, yoga

kicked your ass, you sucked at it, couldn't corpse,

ever the insomniac, fretting you'd fail,

lie down but wouldn't sleep, forever fidgeting

even through your own funeral, incessant restless in the box.

Temperamentally unfit for death, are you? It can't be

outwit. Everyone who's lived has died *so far,* you'd say, ever

nimble. That's it! You're here to stay.

SKELETON

Sorry to text so late but you've

kept me going through this (you, a sweet

elixir tendering me to sleep while kinda

losing my wintry mind).

Enter summer its windblown terrace of light.

Tomorrow it's possible we could bring back laughter, breath,

optimism, reinstate the face-to-face (kisses, flesh—

nothing prepared us for this   how it could all be taken away)

SKELETON

Shabbier I am still a certain person but

kissed less often   more often pissed

excesses rendering fewer blooms

lesser   though not yet a dead thing

equipped still with muscle and skin   even as

time's running   (accept it)

oh   I used to lead with female   aflame—

nonsense now

SKELETON

So after a year undercover wind feels air-

kissed fresh obscene on unmasked skin my face all

eek don't look at me.   The new style of summer's bare-

lipped   & everywhere faces display

eager & flagrant   a stampede of

transgressions.   Sky-air hits mouth-skin like

orgasmic. Seems they'll let us live again &

now all over this city the street fever resumes.

FLESH

The long and short of it is a podcast can only take you so far.

There goes our summer neighbor,

Wife-of-Bath'ing it at the barbecue again,

her toned shoulders, her backtalk and small army of dogs.

Here we still are. Another summer,

same bathing suit. Same cutoffs and blueberries.

The same sordid daydream I keep having, ashamed

here to say because someone might see.

We won't do a single new thing it turns out, just keep cycling

through the years as if they were endless, as if they'd never cease.

Will we ever run out of days? Who dares to count.

To say there are maybe thirty more Christmases,

if we're lucky, thirty more Julys.

SKELETON

Summer dark found us binge-watching the Perseid, perched high

kinked on the lifeguard chair, undertowed by sky. The stars again with their

echolalia, their vanishing. August had come round once more with its compulsory

lusciousness, its tang of berries on the tongue. We preened in preparation,

epilation predictable as rosé, grass stains, mosquito bites, biking at night.

Toddlers thumbed their noses at the pandemic, the sidelined

octogenarians. We tried to stay preoccupied with seasonal frivolities, like how

nano or non were our sunscreens, like flip-flops, tick checks, the cycle of tides.

SKELETON

Sexing sunburned is the worst, sand shrapnel-studding the mattress,

klonopin masking the sting sparking thighs to eyelids.

Effed-up simultaneity as if bringing him off in my mouth while

lashed head to toe by some hothead into this blister of welts.

Eros, Thanatos, we maxed out for years. Who's hating on us now?

Touché. The beach was your idea. Monogamy has its share of

occupational hazards, this we know. Time to mix it up. Come again?

Naughty, wipe yr smile, see how the sun still urges us out, forward.

SKELETON

Slot-machine cherries got nothing on these cherries, pure

kitsch   such plush kerplunk big fruit energy

exists only in Paris, why is that?

louche juice,   farm to mouth,   the sweetest cerise mess.

Eggs à La Palette come raw that's the way they eat them so I do

(triage later but for now choke down this runny yolk ball, ew).

Own the summer vertigo. No mate no snag no shape to these days—

nab this life while you can mad fleet s'il vous plaît.

SKELETON

Skeleton, some wonder if you are practical

keening as you do through this city

ensconced in flesh, a tailored suit for bones

lost plush in skin. Is it a good life within

exiled in the singular anatomical body?

(Thanatophobia, mine.) Ok, breathe. There's

oodles of oxygen for now—let's live a little, we're here!

Natter on, nitwit. I've had about enough of you.

FLESH

You in your ecstasy of coffee me all amped on juice
an ooze of sunshine a foil of water a concordance
two waves in sync making a larger bright
it's unseasonably warm again nothing will bloom
the trees blown way ahead of schedule and we never
kissed not even once despite the come-ons of summer
scented with rain, lilacs in the deli tempting to send me over the edge
as if we could rinse everything and be clean again but no—
Thursday 4 p.m. the city can be beautiful
when it wants to   stands around so photogenic
by the boat pond, lucent doorway of the day
beams us through, pine needles, puddles, tussle
on the sidewalk, a pigeon or two—   streaming by
here come the minutes exposing themselves
and there they go   what is real?
June keeps on flaunting its meadow of music, its drink
let's leave our apartments and go to the park
it's a festival we want a popsicle some honeydew a break
let's go out into the music flowingbroadly now through giant speakers.
The success of friendship let's drink to it—
Hello emptiness that is coming it will engulf
and then, a freighted woman I'll fall back into my hole,
goodbye.   My body will never be satisfied.
But here in the preheadache seasonal glitter,
first burst of summer, still the thrill of it, the heat—

FLESH

I wanted to write the thing itself—
pinned, magnetic,
ambient swoon in the infinite air.
Eros writ large.
Life, the full force of it
pressing us together good and hard.
But. But what?

FLESH

It wouldn't be so bad if it didn't all go on without you.

These inhabited days, the no-see-ums of the fifth arrondissement

that bit us all summer, the hard fact of time hauling us forward lit.

This is the nth year of my life and so far it's not the last

and so far it's not the sweetest but it is because life is sweet.

Swept out with the tide we'll be, beached even

as the mornings keep chirping on and suddenly.

The ten-day weather forecast, the tenth day of rain—we won't be in it.

We will miss the ice storm, we'll be gone before the blizzard,

we'll lie down in the dark forever just bones.

But Monday says off with you ok,

and M is backpacked up and come on boys,

and in the cloth of fall into the wind toward the first day

of September, yielding again forward swept—

into the not young we go awhile before ghosting the old.

Mommy in midlife is she nonperishable? Of course not.

Let's play full speed ahead with the bright souvenirs of this day.

Wasn't I a hapless one. Fundamentally mental.

Watching days go by this life not knowing how to do it.

Watching the boys turn ten then teenaged then.

The new baby girl a surprise that grew up too.

Intricate past numb present and the future that narrows

all of us into a shovel of dirt.

This is my fifth book of poems. I had my way with each of them.

I looked up and I was older than my mother ever ever ever was.

ECSTASIES

I

In the xyzs of nights and days we stayed
as if the conversation would go on forever,
you, you, you—ample days of you,

your beard accumulating a bit of snow,
the gradual showing of bone, a grizzled diminishment.
The stacked-up winters, each in its place.

In this manner the years.
Spooled out the other side as if in plain view—
a field without you.

Meanwhile we took good care, the greens were organic,
honey sweetened the pot, the membrane between us stayed transparent,
and we took seriously our allegiance to dream.

II

Like most people, I am sad at the source.
What is my task then? Tsk. Throb. Begin.
The very best time for the body is in a lighted doorway,

after a snowstorm, in the bathtub with a dog standing by.
The best time for the body is now, aspirational in the same space,
the bed, where we treat ourselves, here, come on, crawl in.

It is quiet here in the room of our insomnia.
The body in its simple existence—lips, thighs, feet.
Birth and love and death, three songs.

Creaks and cricks the skeleton but shush
it's still alive with its hat of hair its cloth of skin its cloak
and scaffolding rickety ribs and spine.

Look, these bones are made for us
and the room is mild, and the catastrophe
though nearer is still not.

III

Are we done with life? I am still so into it.

I like to drink and read and use my mouth

our bodies constellating in the smothering heat

as the trucks slam by, the song of a siren

has a sort of infinity in it, so too the poof

of dove on the sill, dropcloth of sheets, a drench,

the coming dusk, drizzle of sky

its fading and spanning—

days become decades and then—

(We belong to a generation of hideous inattention

clutching our rectangles of light like—

who am I talking to?)

IV

Even coffins oblige   who could stand to lie still

for such a long time? What if I sneeze down there

with everyone else aboveground breathing

what if nothingness is a cold scrape and no more—

oh toast and oranges what are we waiting for,

we are just born, we're on the brink,

let's ravel together while we still have limbs

in this room made warm by our own resources.

Our appetites don't know from time's-up, hurry,

we trample everything we touch, accumulate and decay,

inelegant machinery, often unsteady,

and only ever casually on our way.

Wild and nervy beside the bed I knelt

like someone trapped in the air of the world.

Hey you, you're a body, slow down.

Bring on the filth and joy,

proceed as you will,

inhabit your skin like you're still here.

V

Catch me alive? I am today—swept through the air in a flesh,

thinky-feeling, lugging itself up the subway stairs

& now back on Spring Street again in the dazing light

pumping the marrow a breeze of breath a blood

& still the minutes accelerate & we wake backweighted

with days will we waste them all & then when we get there

we will think I wasted them all, stony before I was laid

in stone, mourning before I was mourned

& what was this velvet for? spring didn't know—

flags of the grave? well also a jubilance not just a bawling

& off again toward whatever, drinking exalted or coughing

but still can swallow & here all your parts are warm & mostly work

& look it's luck, while not yet a word from the underworld,

the necklace of days bracelets of hours the flush of blood

present swelling the yes please of sex the abject of—

is it precarious yes exquisite *alive*, staging its trance

the hand in hand, the mouth sloshed with coffee, sugared & warm,

your silent reading this now.

ABOUT THE AUTHOR

Deborah Landau is the author of five collections of poetry. Her honors include a Guggenheim Fellowship and the Believer Book Award. She is a professor at New York University, where she directs the Creative Writing Program, and she lives in Brooklyn.

Poetry is vital to language and living. Since 1972, Copper Canyon Press has published extraordinary poetry from around the world to engage the imaginations and intellects of readers, writers, booksellers, librarians, teachers, students, and donors.

WE ARE GRATEFUL FOR THE MAJOR SUPPORT PROVIDED BY:

Richard Andrews and Colleen Chartier
Anonymous
Jill Baker and Jeffrey Bishop
Anne and Geoffrey Barker
Donna Bellew
Matthew Bellew
Sarah Bird
Will Blythe
John Branch
Diana Broze
Sarah Cavanaugh
Keith Cowan and Linda Walsh
Stephanie Ellis-Smith and
    Douglas Smith
Mimi Gardner Gates
Gull Industries Inc. on behalf of
    William True
The Trust of Warren A. Gummow
William R. Hearst III
Carolyn and Robert Hedin
David and Jane Hibbard
Bruce S. Kahn
Phil Kovacevich and Eric Wechsler
Lakeside Industries Inc. on behalf of
    Jeanne Marie Lee

Maureen Lee and Mark Busto
Peter Lewis and Johanna Turiano
Ellie Mathews and Carl Youngmann as
    The North Press
Larry Mawby and Lois Bahle
Hank and Liesel Meijer
Jack Nicholson
Petunia Charitable Fund and
    adviser Elizabeth Hebert
Madelyn Pitts
Suzanne Rapp and Mark Hamilton
Adam and Lynn Rauch
Emily and Dan Raymond
Joseph C. Roberts
Jill and Bill Ruckelshaus
Cynthia Sears
Kim and Jeff Seely
Nora Hutton Shepard
D.D. Wigley
Joan F. Woods
Barbara and Charles Wright
In honor of C.D. Wright,
    from Forrest Gander
Caleb Young as C. Young Creative
The dedicated interns and faithful
    volunteers of Copper Canyon Press

TO LEARN MORE ABOUT UNDERWRITING COPPER CANYON PRESS TITLES,
PLEASE CALL 360-385-4925 EXT. 103

The pressmark for Copper Canyon Press
suggests entrance, connection, and interaction
while holding at its center
an attentive, dynamic space for poetry.

This book is set in Acumin Pro and Adobe Caslon Pro.
Book design by Phil Kovacevich.
Printed on archival-quality paper.